THE
CARROT
TRACKER

THE
CARROT
TRACKER

The Ultimate Tool for Motivating
Your Employees with Recognition

Adrian Gostick and **Chester Elton**

authors of *New York Times* bestseller *The Carrot Principle*

CHRONICLE BOOKS
SAN FRANCISCO

ISBN: 978-0-8118-7680-3

Manufactured in China
Designed by Jennifer Tolo Pierce
Typeset in Berthold Akzidenz Grotesk
and Warnock Pro

is a registered trademark of O.C. Tanner Company.

10 9 8 7 6 5 4 3 2 1

Chronicle Books LLC
680 Second Street
San Francisco, California 94107
www.chroniclebooks.com

INTRODUCTION

We once spent an hour in the hospital, visiting an elderly friend who had fallen ill. We sat down by his bed and briefly talked about his condition, but that didn't hold his interest for long. He had something else on his mind.

Holding up a small stack of photos he'd been looking at when we came in, he motioned us closer. We leaned in, expecting that at this difficult time, he'd be comforted by pictures of his late wife or his grandchildren. To our surprise, we found ourselves staring at photos of flowers and plants. "I'm trying lilies in my front beds this year," he said. "And I think I'll get 40 pints of tomatoes from my garden," he flipped the photo over to show us the pencil marks he'd tallied on the back.

Now, we'd always known that Roy's garden was important to him; but until that moment we didn't realize how important it was. Away from home, and gravely ill, he kept records of his rose bushes, chrysanthemums, and bean crop close at hand, and close to his heart.

We're all like Roy, in a way: We record what is important, and hold on to it. Birth records, college diplomas, marriage certificates. When you think about it, all of the most important events and achievements in our lives are recorded somewhere as proof that they happened.

For many years now, we have preserved the moments that have had the most impact on our personal and business lives through journals. Our journals are filled with event tickets, foreign currency, and pictures of celebrations with new friends around the world. Although they started as simply a labor of love, along the way we discovered a business case for journals that we didn't anticipate: *Journals are powerful recognition tools.*

On one level, they help us to remember the times we have excelled. The ability to instantly relive the moments you thought you'd never forget (but, inevitably you do) is priceless enough. Like the time we had to drive all night to make a presentation when the flight was canceled, or the time we met a manager who had taken his department's customer satisfaction scores from worst to best in the country in six months—these moments are all inscribed in our journals, and when we read our thoughts, we feel like the events happened just an hour ago. And the more often we relive the positive emotions associated with those times, the more motivated we are to repeat them.

On another level, our journals have prompted us to more frequently recognize those around us. As we record experiences or read through previous entries, it jogs our memories about additional people who deserve our thanks. There's no doubt that the bits and pieces we scribble in our books help us to be more accountable to appreciate the people in our lives who display brilliance, persistence, passion, and teamwork.

We're hoping *The Carrot Tracker* will serve a similar purpose for you—that the act of planning, recording, and remembering important events to celebrate will inspire you toward your finest moments as a leader. It will also help you build a work environment where people want to come every day and give their very best. We call this a culture of appreciation, or a Carrot Culture.

We hope you will use this little book to record, celebrate, and create memories of the wonderful things your team accomplishes each day. Our wish also is that at the end of every year you will smile as you page through your journal, reliving all the positive moments and great victories that were so hard-won.

After all, important events *should* be recorded. Get in the habit of recording and appreciating the moments that impact your work life, and soon you'll find that those positive memories will burn brighter over time, becoming part of the legacy of your teams and organizations. You will find, as we have, that you are building your own traditions of caring and winning.

Good luck and good writing.

"Everyone has an invisible sign hanging from their neck saying, 'Make me feel important.'"

–MARY KAY ASH, *Mary Kay cosmetics*

HOW TO USE THE JOURNAL

Recognition is about remembering what happened yesterday. But it's also about something more. In the hands of a skillful leader, remembering the past is a way to create a better future.

Some managers miss the point of recognition and view it as touchy-feely stuff. But there's a reason that this concept of appreciation thrives in some of the most disciplined and successful organizations in the world: Recognition is more than simply being nice; it encourages employees to move their team or company toward its goals.

And that means we must praise well-intentioned efforts—even if the results aren't perfect—because the employees you recognize are trying to advance the ball. We need to reward great results, because when no one says "thanks" when we go above and beyond, we rarely attempt such heroics again.

As managers, we must learn to celebrate even when it doesn't look like there is much to celebrate. Why? Because the goal is to move employees forward from wherever they are right now—inspiring new behaviors that will impact your team, your organization, or even your industry—beyond your wildest imagination.

Enter the Recognition Tracker

This guide will take you step-by-step through the process of noting above-and-beyond achievements, planning an appropriate recognition moment, and tracking those events for each employee throughout the year. It will give you greater confidence to cheer for your colleagues and will allow you to better communicate your company's vision to employees. As you develop these skills, you'll find that team members will have an increased capacity to meet company values and priorities, giving you more and more reasons to celebrate.

The first step in this journey is to understand how to note recognition-worthy events. The great managers we've studied spend at least part of every day with their employees, asking about challenges and successes, and encouraging their progress. These managers maintain a notebook to capture thoughts and to remember accomplishments. For instance:

* Erica had to stay late yesterday finishing that order, and I think she missed her kid's baseball game.

* Jeremy had a great idea for a new way to inventory. This is going to save us a lot of time and money.

* Donna offered to pick up an extra shift this weekend—she always shows great teamwork.

Make a detailed account of each achievement in the Recognition Tracker section of this journal.

Then it's time to set SAIL.

SAIL

To make a memorable recognition presentation, you are going to need to tell a story. Don't worry if you are not a raconteur—we can help. During the most powerful award presentations, the presenter covers four basics: *Situation, Action, Impact,* and *Link*. We call it SAIL, for short.

The acronym is appropriate, since it implies movement toward a predetermined destination. SAIL connects the rewarded behavior to how it fits into the company values, keeping everyone on course toward shared goals. The following pages introduce you to how to implement SAIL.

Situation: In the space provided in this journal, describe the challenge or opportunity that the employee faced. It's not necessary to embellish; sincerity and accuracy are most important. It's also essential not to bluff. The goal is to let people know how the company or team could have been impacted by the situation. You'll use this journal during the presentation to help you remember dates and numbers. If you're not sure of the details, either take the time to find out or have someone closer to the action make the presentation. You might write something like:

* November 15. Kim Lindstrom with VestaTech, an important customer, called to say that she was angry that a shipment was delayed.

Action: In this section, describe, in specific terms, what the employee did and what that action achieved. General praise, such as "She did a great job," leaves coworkers wondering how to replicate the behavior. And it leaves them wondering if you, the boss, really know what's going on. Make it clear:

* Sharon took ownership of the problem. She calmed the client down and said that she would not hang up until she found out where the shipment was and what could be done to get it to the client the same day. I know she had a hundred things on her desk, but it was clear to the client that nothing was as important as rectifying the situation.

These specific descriptions of employee achievements demonstrate that awards are based on merit, not favoritism.

Impact: Next, you'll describe the impact of the action. Quantifying the result with numbers is ideal:

* Rob's streamlined approach reduced two days in processing time.

But that might not always be possible. Customer or coworker quotes can bring the impact to life:

* Joan at Harvington called me after she spoke with Sharon. She was very impressed with how Sharon took charge and made her feel at ease.

Even descriptions of what you observed are valid:

* I was so impressed with how Brian calmed that upset patient in the midst of a very busy ER.

Link: Finally, you'll bring this all together by describing how the achievement aligns with company values:

* Sharon demonstrated one of our core values around here: *Ownership*. We don't pass the buck, we own problems when they occur.

This is the step most leaders miss; so while their recognition is nice, it's not strategic. General or vague praise does not move the team toward the next milestone.

We like to say that the celebration of one success launches a thousand more—but only if you set a clear course. Recognition moments are the ideal time to remind employees of what the company values most. After all, no one tunes out during an award presentation: not the person getting the award and certainly not the team members who are trying to figure out how to be the next one recognized. Do this enough, and employees should be able to recite your values in their sleep. That's a good thing, because employees familiar with company goals are better able to prioritize their activities. In essence, you are giving them the skills to improve their future performance.

It's important to note that many awards feature a symbolic link to the company, such as a corporate logo crafted in precious metals with gems. The Link section is the perfect time to speak about the symbolism of the logo and the award itself—taking the time to symbolically connect the employee to the company through the award immediately ratchets up recognition's perceived value.

Inviting Colleagues to Participate

Recognition is a validating process for your employees. It proves that the good things they see in themselves are not just wishful thinking; others see and appreciate them too. And recognition is particularly effective when it comes from the people whose opinions they value most: their direct supervisors and close colleagues.

With this in mind, it is usually not a good idea to invite a senior-level manager to make the presentation unless he or she has direct knowledge of the specific achievement. We've seen these award ceremonies go very wrong as these well-intentioned leaders mess up details or even the employee's name. Instead, we highly recommend inviting one or two close colleagues of the employee to participate in the award presentation with you. Not only will their participation validate the employee, it also gives these coworkers a taste of how good it feels to recognize someone else. Peer-to-peer recognition is incredibly rare and amazingly potent. Take the chance to encourage it as often as you can (some leaders even provide a stack of thank-you notes to facilitate this type of recognition between coworkers).

You should coach everyone to avoid any negativity or sarcasm (even in jest) during recognition moments. People may think they're being funny; but teasing is hurtful, especially during such an openly emotional moment. Only the positive should be addressed. The rule is: We praise in public and correct in private.

Choosing an Award

Selecting the right award will be an enduring symbol of the employee's achievement and your regard for him or her. We learned recently of a retiree who requested that, when the time comes, she be buried wearing the jewelry item she received at her retirement award presentation.

At the other extreme is the manager who admitted that when she recognizes employees, she never gives more than a bag of candy. This misguided manager added that she always attaches a bow to the candy "to make it more significant." Nothing more is needed, she told us. Now, there are times when a company mug, T-shirt, or even a bag of candy with a bow are appropriate for on-the-spot thanks; but these awards are hardly recompense for an above-and-beyond achievement. The key is to ensure that awards are equitable, meaning that they are appropriate in value and symbolism to the achievement.

Following are some ideas to get you started, but remember it's most important to be creative and personalize rewards for each employee. Overall, awards can be classified into several categories:

Praise: In the most productive work teams, employees feel praised for their efforts at least once every seven days. Obviously you aren't handing out Rolex watches or trips to Hawaii with such frequency. Instead, the most appreciation that an employee will receive will be face-to-face. You'll offer specific, public verbal encouragement and thanks. Make an effort to vary the way you deliver this praise. In person is best. Handwritten letters and notes of thanks are always heartfelt and well received. And now and then you can certainly include an e-mail or voicemail of praise.

On-the-spot Awards: Once every month or two an employee should be deserving of a low-cost award to recognize actions that move her a small step toward strengthening company values. In short, aim to frequently reward the behaviors you want repeated. By doing so, you demonstrate to employees which activities are most important. An employee might qualify for this type of recognition by staying late or working an extra shift, providing a good idea that helps a project, demonstrating strong teamwork or dependability, and so on. Awards in this category may include movie tickets, cafeteria passes, gift cards to a local coffee shop, or small items that may be meaningful to the employee (her preferred snack, dinner at his favorite restaurant, etc.).

Above and Beyond: When employees achieve significant results, they should receive a tangible award that appropriately thanks them. These awards provide a structured way to reward achievements that further the company's core values and goals—whether the accomplishment of a sales goal, the implementation of a smart idea, providing exceptional customer service, and so on. When employees rise to a challenge, reward their achievements in a public way with a meaningful reminder of the accomplishment. This doesn't mean providing them with cash; it means finding a palpable award (or a choice from a selection of items) that they will appreciate and treasure. Research shows that people work harder for items that they can see themselves using: a new mountain bike, flat-screen television, jewelry item, or set of golf clubs.

Milestones: Most companies have a service anniversary program, but most of these programs take too long to kick in. If you look at employment statistics, most turnover happens in the first eighteen months of employment. Naturally, if you want to hold on to workers, you can't wait five years to recognize them—chances are, they won't be around. We recommend starting at ninety days and using SAIL to recognize an employee's early contributions and the things that he or she has brought to the job. Done right, employees will be around not only for their one-year service anniversary (where you'll present another symbolic award), but for their three-year, five-year, seven-year, and 10-year awards—and all the way up to a meaningful retirement award. It's important to remember that the best milestone awards are items that are lasting in nature and are designed to be displayed. For instance, a clock or writing instrument is more appropriate for a service award than a sleeping bag or a barbecue.

Team Celebrations: Winning teams celebrate not only the big victories but also small milestones along the way. These team celebrations reinforce your values and thank everyone collectively for their hard work.

Team awards and events aren't replacements for individual recognition but complement your other efforts and help bring a sense of camaraderie to the group. Events to celebrate include the completion of a project, achievement of record-setting results, company anniversaries, new product launches, and so on.

The Right Award

We've seen a mountain of inappropriate awards in our time. There was the manager who generously handed out hams before the Christmas holiday, only to later realize that several of his employees were Jewish. We'll also never forget the company that gave its top sales producer a trip to a tropical island, only to discover a year later that he had never used the excursion due to his paralyzing fear of flying. And who would not cringe when watching a CEO reward his workforce for completing a grueling six-month certification process with a stack of cheap plastic mugs. We could go on . . . and on.

Please, don't add to the heap of shameful, wasted awards. The answer? If you can't offer a company-sponsored selection of awards, then get to know your employees and find out what they would value. Start by writing down what you know about your employee's likes and dislikes. If you need more information, ask coworkers and ask the employee him- or herself. As you learn more about each employee, write your thoughts down in the Employee Log section at the back of this journal. You might think you'll remember such details as her preferred sweet treat or his favorite musician, but you won't. You'll find yourself returning to your notes again and again as you continue to provide recognition awards that will be personally meaningful to an employee.

Many will say that they are motivated only by the almighty dollar. The danger with cash, however, is that it immediately quantifies an achievement. For instance, an employee may begin to think: "Oh,

I guess the extra weekends I spent on that project were worth 50 bucks." In addition, money is not memorable. Small amounts are used to pay down the gas bill or credit card debt. A month later, the vast majority of employees can't remember what they did with the cash. However, a considerate award has trophy value; each time the employee sees it, he is reminded of his achievement and the company's regard for him. A meaningful award is also more difficult to define with a dollar value. How can one put a price on the thoughtfulness of a helmet cam for the avid bicyclist, the new Stephen King novel for the raving fan, or dinner downtown for the gourmand?

We've found that some of the most effective awards are those that help an employee overcome personal challenges or meet individual goals. Particularly touching was a leader who paid for tutoring sessions for an employee's child. The lessons were beyond the employee's budget, and she'd been agonizing over how to cover the cost. The award brought her (and everyone else in the room) to tears. Standing there, everyone realized that to give such a personally meaningful gift, the manager must have invested the time to know what motivated the employee.

At times you may need a little inspiration to find effective rewards. If you're stuck, peruse the list of ideas at Carrots.com. Or ask your friends and colleagues about their most memorable recognition moments; also recall praise that's stuck with you over the years.

Remember that whatever award you ultimately select, you can immediately boost the perceived value by adding a symbolic element. This could be the corporate logo or your team's mascot. Some teams create a unique symbol to use just for achievement awards. You can magnify the impact by speaking about the symbolism of the award as you present it to the employee.

Employee Log

As you complete each recognition experience, take a moment to record it in the Employee Log at the back of this journal. Keeping the logs updated will allow you to see at a glance how you are doing at recognizing each employee, helping to ensure no one on your staff is neglected.

Perhaps most important, the Log will serve as a wonderful tool during performance reviews. Instead of asking, "So what did you accomplish this year?" you'll be able to talk about his or her accomplishments in vivid detail.

Perfect Timing

In our surveys of great workplaces, managers don't spend an inordinate amount of time engaged in recognition. Great leaders typically devote about an hour of their time each week to recognition, or just 2 percent of a 50-hour workweek. So time is on your side. Even the most memorable recognition moments don't take more than a few minutes; but for an employee, the memory can last a lifetime.

Timeliness matters. Remember that layers of approvals and long delays kill recognition's impact. Keep the recognition process simple, strategic, and, most of all, close to the action. There's a reason sports leagues award their trophies right after the championship games, when the sweat is still streaming down athletes' faces: Appreciation means more right after the event.

Now you are ready to get started. Remember:

* Note recognition-worthy events right away.
* Make meaningful presentations using SAIL.
* Choose awards that will have a personal impact.
* Involve others.
* Don't forget to log everything as you go.

Using this journal will change the way you lead your team. In the process of striving to improve our employees, we cannot help but dramatically improve ourselves. You will start to see the world in a more positive light. You will see how many people around you help in achieving your goals. And you'll begin to shape the future.

"I have yet to find a man, however exalted his station, who did not do better work and put forth greater effort under a spirit of approval than under a spirit of criticism."

–CHARLES SCHWAB

RECOGNITION TRACKER

PRESENTATION PREPARATION

Name/Event: ....

Date: ....

Value being recognized: ....

Tell a story using SAIL

* Situation *(the problem or opportunity)*:

....

....

....

....

* Action *(what was done, in specific terms)*:

....

....

....

....

* Impact *(the result of the action)*:

....

....

....

....

* Link *(how the action contributed to the company)*:

....

....

....

....

RECOGNITION GIVEN

Recognition ideas:

- ○ Handwritten thank-you note
- ○ Company performance recognition award
- ○ Personalized certificate or plaque
- ○ Training class or seminar

- ○ Event ticket (sports or arts)
- ○ Media: DVD, CD, etc.
- ○ Restaurant gift certificate
- ○ Movie passes
- ○ Other: ....

"If businesses are to grow . . . they will have to get more productivity out of their people—not by cutting and slashing, but by nurturing, engaging, and recognizing."

–JOHN A. BYRNE, *editor in chief*, Fast Company *magazine*

Don't forget to record this recognition moment in the Employee Log.

ADDITIONAL NOTES

PRESENTATION PREPARATION

Name/Event: ....

Date: ....

Value being recognized: ....

Tell a story using SAIL

✳ Situation *(the problem or opportunity)*:

....

....

....

....

✳ Action *(what was done, in specific terms)*:

....

....

....

....

✳ Impact *(the result of the action)*:

....

....

....

....

✳ Link *(how the action contributed to the company)*:

....

....

....

....

RECOGNITION GIVEN

Recognition ideas:

- Handwritten thank-you note
- Company performance recognition award
- Personalized certificate or plaque
- Training class or seminar

- Event ticket (sports or arts)
- Media: DVD, CD, etc.
- Restaurant gift certificate
- Movie passes
- Other: ....

 Don't forget to record this recognition moment in the Employee Log.

ADDITIONAL NOTES

PRESENTATION PREPARATION

Name/Event: ....

Date: ....

Value being recognized: ....

Tell a story using SAIL

✽ Situation *(the problem or opportunity)*:

....

....

....

....

✽ Action *(what was done, in specific terms)*:

....

....

....

....

✽ Impact *(the result of the action)*:

....

....

....

....

✽ Link *(how the action contributed to the company)*:

....

....

....

....

RECOGNITION GIVEN

Recognition ideas:

- ○ Handwritten thank-you note
- ○ Company performance recognition award
- ○ Personalized certificate or plaque
- ○ Training class or seminar

- ○ Event ticket (sports or arts)
- ○ Media: DVD, CD, etc.
- ○ Restaurant gift certificate
- ○ Movie passes
- ○ Other: ....

"The celebration of one success launches a thousand more."

–ADRIAN GOSTICK and **CHESTER ELTON,** *authors*

Don't forget to record this recognition moment in the Employee Log.

ADDITIONAL NOTES

PRESENTATION PREPARATION

Name/Event: ....

Date: ....

Value being recognized: ....

Tell a story using SAIL

* Situation *(the problem or opportunity)*:

....

....

....

....

* Action *(what was done, in specific terms)*:

....

....

....

....

* Impact *(the result of the action)*:

....

....

....

....

* Link *(how the action contributed to the company)*:

....

....

....

....

RECOGNITION GIVEN

Recognition ideas:

- ○ Handwritten thank-you note
- ○ Company performance recognition award
- ○ Personalized certificate or plaque
- ○ Training class or seminar

- ○ Event ticket (sports or arts)
- ○ Media: DVD, CD, etc.
- ○ Restaurant gift certificate
- ○ Movie passes
- ○ Other: ....

Don't forget to record this recognition moment in the Employee Log.

ADDITIONAL NOTES

PRESENTATION PREPARATION

Name/Event: ....

Date: ....

Value being recognized: ....

Tell a story using SAIL

* Situation *(the problem or opportunity)*:

....

....

....

....

* Action *(what was done, in specific terms)*:

....

....

....

....

* Impact *(the result of the action)*:

....

....

....

....

* Link *(how the action contributed to the company)*:

....

....

....

....

RECOGNITION GIVEN

Recognition ideas:

- Handwritten thank-you note
- Company performance recognition award
- Personalized certificate or plaque
- Training class or seminar

- Event ticket (sports or arts)
- Media: DVD, CD, etc.
- Restaurant gift certificate
- Movie passes
- Other: ....

" American business is fast discovering that monetary rewards are not only very costly, they are extremely limited in their ability to motivate employees."

-WAYNE SLOUGH, *Center for Organizational Effectiveness*

Don't forget to record this recognition moment in the Employee Log.

ADDITIONAL NOTES

PRESENTATION PREPARATION

Name/Event: ....

Date: ....

Value being recognized: ....

Tell a story using SAIL

*   Situation *(the problem or opportunity)*:

....

....

....

....

*   Action *(what was done, in specific terms)*:

....

....

....

....

*   Impact *(the result of the action)*:

....

....

....

....

*   Link *(how the action contributed to the company)*:

....

....

....

....

RECOGNITION GIVEN

Recognition ideas:

- ○ Handwritten thank-you note
- ○ Company performance recognition award
- ○ Personalized certificate or plaque
- ○ Training class or seminar

- ○ Event ticket (sports or arts)
- ○ Media: DVD, CD, etc.
- ○ Restaurant gift certificate
- ○ Movie passes
- ○ Other:..

Don't forget to record this recognition moment in the Employee Log.

ADDITIONAL NOTES

PRESENTATION PREPARATION

Name/Event: ....

Date: ....

Value being recognized: ....

Tell a story using SAIL

✱ Situation *(the problem or opportunity)*:

....

....

....

....

✱ Action *(what was done, in specific terms)*:

....

....

....

....

✱ Impact *(the result of the action)*:

....

....

....

....

✱ Link *(how the action contributed to the company)*:

....

....

....

....

RECOGNITION GIVEN

Recognition ideas:

- ○ Handwritten thank-you note
- ○ Company performance recognition award
- ○ Personalized certificate or plaque
- ○ Training class or seminar
- ○ Event ticket (sports or arts)
- ○ Media: DVD, CD, etc.
- ○ Restaurant gift certificate
- ○ Movie passes
- ○ Other: ....

"We applaud each little success one after another—and the first thing you know, they actually become successful. We praise them to success!"

–MARY KAY ASH, *founder, Mary Kay cosmetics*

Don't forget to record this recognition moment in the Employee Log.

ADDITIONAL NOTES

PRESENTATION PREPARATION

Name/Event: ....

Date: ....

Value being recognized: ....

Tell a story using SAIL

✱ Situation *(the problem or opportunity)*:

....

....

....

....

✱ Action *(what was done, in specific terms)*:

....

....

....

....

✱ Impact *(the result of the action)*:

....

....

....

....

✱ Link *(how the action contributed to the company)*:

....

....

....

....

RECOGNITION GIVEN

Recognition ideas:

- Handwritten thank-you note
- Company performance recognition award
- Personalized certificate or plaque
- Training class or seminar

- Event ticket (sports or arts)
- Media: DVD, CD, etc.
- Restaurant gift certificate
- Movie passes
- Other: ....

Don't forget to record this recognition moment in the Employee Log.

ADDITIONAL NOTES

PRESENTATION PREPARATION

Name/Event: ....

Date: ....

Value being recognized: ....

Tell a story using SAIL

*   Situation *(the problem or opportunity):*

....

....

....

....

*   Action *(what was done, in specific terms):*

....

....

....

....

*   Impact *(the result of the action):*

....

....

....

....

*   Link *(how the action contributed to the company):*

....

....

....

....

RECOGNITION GIVEN

Recognition ideas:

- ○ Handwritten thank-you note
- ○ Company performance recognition award
- ○ Personalized certificate or plaque
- ○ Training class or seminar

- ○ Event ticket (sports or arts)
- ○ Media: DVD, CD, etc.
- ○ Restaurant gift certificate
- ○ Movie passes
- ○ Other: ....

"We communicate with the masses, but we manage to the one."

–ADRIAN GOSTICK and CHESTER ELTON, *authors*

Don't forget to record this recognition moment in the Employee Log.

ADDITIONAL NOTES

PRESENTATION PREPARATION

Name/Event: ....

Date: ....

Value being recognized: ....

Tell a story using SAIL

✱   Situation *(the problem or opportunity)*:

....

....

....

....

✱   Action *(what was done, in specific terms)*:

....

....

....

....

✱   Impact *(the result of the action)*:

....

....

....

....

✱   Link *(how the action contributed to the company)*:

....

....

....

....

RECOGNITION GIVEN

Recognition ideas:

○ Handwritten thank-you note

○ Company performance
recognition award

○ Personalized certificate
or plaque

○ Training class or seminar

○ Event ticket (sports or arts)

○ Media: DVD, CD, etc.

○ Restaurant gift certificate

○ Movie passes

○ Other:..

Don't forget to record this recognition moment in the Employee Log.

ADDITIONAL NOTES

PRESENTATION PREPARATION

Name/Event: ....

Date: ....

Value being recognized: ....

Tell a story using SAIL

✱   Situation *(the problem or opportunity)*:

....

....

....

....

✱   Action *(what was done, in specific terms)*:

....

....

....

....

✱   Impact *(the result of the action)*:

....

....

....

....

✱   Link *(how the action contributed to the company)*:

....

....

....

....

RECOGNITION GIVEN

Recognition ideas:

- ○ Handwritten thank-you note
- ○ Company performance recognition award
- ○ Personalized certificate or plaque
- ○ Training class or seminar
- ○ Event ticket (sports or arts)
- ○ Media: DVD, CD, etc.
- ○ Restaurant gift certificate
- ○ Movie passes
- ○ Other: ....

"Recognition is like a small drop of oil in the machinery of business . . . it just makes things run a little smoother."

–OBERT C. TANNER, *founder, O.C. Tanner Co., employee recognition industry*

Don't forget to record this recognition moment in the Employee Log.

ADDITIONAL NOTES

PRESENTATION PREPARATION

Name/Event: ....

Date: ....

Value being recognized: ....

Tell a story using SAIL

* Situation *(the problem or opportunity)*:

....

....

....

....

* Action *(what was done, in specific terms)*:

....

....

....

....

* Impact *(the result of the action)*:

....

....

....

....

* Link *(how the action contributed to the company)*:

....

....

....

....

RECOGNITION GIVEN

Recognition ideas:

- ○ Handwritten thank-you note
- ○ Company performance recognition award
- ○ Personalized certificate or plaque
- ○ Training class or seminar

- ○ Event ticket (sports or arts)
- ○ Media: DVD, CD, etc.
- ○ Restaurant gift certificate
- ○ Movie passes
- ○ Other: ....

Don't forget to record this recognition moment in the Employee Log.

ADDITIONAL NOTES

PRESENTATION PREPARATION

Name/Event:..

Date:..

Value being recognized:...

Tell a story using SAIL

    ✳ Situation *(the problem or opportunity)*:

....

....

....

....

    ✳ Action *(what was done, in specific terms)*:

....

....

....

....

    ✳ Impact *(the result of the action)*:

....

....

....

....

    ✳ Link *(how the action contributed to the company)*:

....

....

....

....

RECOGNITION GIVEN

Recognition ideas:

- ○ Handwritten thank-you note
- ○ Company performance recognition award
- ○ Personalized certificate or plaque
- ○ Training class or seminar
- ○ Event ticket (sports or arts)
- ○ Media: DVD, CD, etc.
- ○ Restaurant gift certificate
- ○ Movie passes
- ○ Other: ....

"You can't know employees as individuals until you're willing to put in the time to talk to them. And you have to talk to know what motivates them."

–ARTHUR R. PELL, *author,* The Complete Idiot's Guide to Managing People

Don't forget to record this recognition moment in the Employee Log.

ADDITIONAL NOTES

PRESENTATION PREPARATION

Name/Event: ....

Date: ....

Value being recognized: ....

Tell a story using SAIL

> ✻ Situation *(the problem or opportunity)*:

....

....

....

....

> ✻ Action *(what was done, in specific terms)*:

....

....

....

....

> ✻ Impact *(the result of the action)*:

....

....

....

....

> ✻ Link *(how the action contributed to the company)*:

....

....

....

....

RECOGNITION GIVEN

Recognition ideas:

- ○ Handwritten thank-you note
- ○ Company performance recognition award
- ○ Personalized certificate or plaque
- ○ Training class or seminar
- ○ Event ticket (sports or arts)
- ○ Media: DVD, CD, etc.
- ○ Restaurant gift certificate
- ○ Movie passes
- ○ Other: ....

Don't forget to record this recognition moment in the Employee Log.

ADDITIONAL NOTES

PRESENTATION PREPARATION

Name/Event: ....

Date: ....

Value being recognized: ....

Tell a story using SAIL

* Situation *(the problem or opportunity)*:

....

....

....

....

* Action *(what was done, in specific terms)*:

....

....

....

....

* Impact *(the result of the action)*:

....

....

....

....

* Link *(how the action contributed to the company)*:

....

....

....

....

RECOGNITION GIVEN

Recognition ideas:

- Handwritten thank-you note
- Company performance recognition award
- Personalized certificate or plaque
- Training class or seminar

- Event ticket (sports or arts)
- Media: DVD, CD, etc.
- Restaurant gift certificate
- Movie passes
- Other: ....

"Praise must be frequent. Employees need to receive some form of recognition every seven days."

—ADRIAN GOSTICK and CHESTER ELTON, *authors*

Don't forget to record this recognition moment in the Employee Log.

ADDITIONAL NOTES

PRESENTATION PREPARATION

Name/Event: ....

Date: ....

Value being recognized: ....

Tell a story using SAIL

* Situation *(the problem or opportunity)*:

....

....

....

....

* Action *(what was done, in specific terms)*:

....

....

....

....

* Impact *(the result of the action)*:

....

....

....

....

* Link *(how the action contributed to the company)*:

....

....

....

....

RECOGNITION GIVEN

Recognition ideas:

- ○ Handwritten thank-you note
- ○ Company performance recognition award
- ○ Personalized certificate or plaque
- ○ Training class or seminar

- ○ Event ticket (sports or arts)
- ○ Media: DVD, CD, etc.
- ○ Restaurant gift certificate
- ○ Movie passes
- ○ Other: ....

Don't forget to record this recognition moment in the Employee Log.

ADDITIONAL NOTES

PRESENTATION PREPARATION

Name/Event: ....

Date: ....

Value being recognized: ....

Tell a story using SAIL

* Situation *(the problem or opportunity)*:

....

....

....

....

* Action *(what was done, in specific terms)*:

....

....

....

....

* Impact *(the result of the action)*:

....

....

....

....

* Link *(how the action contributed to the company)*:

....

....

....

....

RECOGNITION GIVEN

Recognition ideas:

- ○ Handwritten thank-you note
- ○ Company performance recognition award
- ○ Personalized certificate or plaque
- ○ Training class or seminar

- ○ Event ticket (sports or arts)
- ○ Media: DVD, CD, etc.
- ○ Restaurant gift certificate
- ○ Movie passes
- ○ Other:...

"According to the American Psychological Association, 'equitable rewards and recognition' are one of the top 12 most essential characteristics for a healthy company culture."

–*WORKFORCE MANAGEMENT* MAGAZINE

Don't forget to record this recognition moment in the Employee Log.

ADDITIONAL NOTES

PRESENTATION PREPARATION

Name/Event: ....

Date: ....

Value being recognized: ....

Tell a story using SAIL

*   Situation *(the problem or opportunity)*:

....

....

....

....

*   Action *(what was done, in specific terms)*:

....

....

....

....

*   Impact *(the result of the action)*:

....

....

....

....

*   Link *(how the action contributed to the company)*:

....

....

....

....

RECOGNITION GIVEN

Recognition ideas:

- Handwritten thank-you note
- Company performance recognition award
- Personalized certificate or plaque
- Training class or seminar

- Event ticket (sports or arts)
- Media: DVD, CD, etc.
- Restaurant gift certificate
- Movie passes
- Other: ....

Don't forget to record this recognition moment in the Employee Log.

ADDITIONAL NOTES

PRESENTATION PREPARATION

Name/Event: ....

Date: ....

Value being recognized: ....

Tell a story using SAIL

*   Situation *(the problem or opportunity)*:

....

....

....

....

*   Action *(what was done, in specific terms)*:

....

....

....

....

*   Impact *(the result of the action)*:

....

....

....

....

*   Link *(how the action contributed to the company)*:

....

....

....

....

RECOGNITION GIVEN

Recognition ideas:

- ○ Handwritten thank-you note
- ○ Company performance recognition award
- ○ Personalized certificate or plaque
- ○ Training class or seminar

- ○ Event ticket (sports or arts)
- ○ Media: DVD, CD, etc.
- ○ Restaurant gift certificate
- ○ Movie passes
- ○ Other: ....

"In the most innovative companies, there is a significantly higher volume of thank-yous than in companies of low innovation."

–ROSABETH MOSS KANTER, *professor, Harvard Business School*

Don't forget to record this recognition moment in the Employee Log.

ADDITIONAL NOTES

PRESENTATION PREPARATION

Name/Event:...

Date:...

Value being recognized:...

Tell a story using SAIL

* Situation *(the problem or opportunity)*:

....

....

....

....

* Action *(what was done, in specific terms)*:

....

....

....

....

* Impact *(the result of the action)*:

....

....

....

....

* Link *(how the action contributed to the company)*:

....

....

....

....

RECOGNITION GIVEN

Recognition ideas:

- ○ Handwritten thank-you note
- ○ Company performance recognition award
- ○ Personalized certificate or plaque
- ○ Training class or seminar

- ○ Event ticket (sports or arts)
- ○ Media: DVD, CD, etc.
- ○ Restaurant gift certificate
- ○ Movie passes
- ○ Other: ....

Don't forget to record this recognition moment in the Employee Log.

ADDITIONAL NOTES

PRESENTATION PREPARATION

Name/Event:..

Date:...

Value being recognized:..

Tell a story using SAIL

✿ Situation *(the problem or opportunity)*:

....

....

....

....

✿ Action *(what was done, in specific terms)*:

....

....

....

....

✿ Impact *(the result of the action)*:

....

....

....

....

✿ Link *(how the action contributed to the company)*:

....

....

....

....

RECOGNITION GIVEN

Recognition ideas:

- ○ Handwritten thank-you note
- ○ Company performance recognition award
- ○ Personalized certificate or plaque
- ○ Training class or seminar
- ○ Event ticket (sports or arts)
- ○ Media: DVD, CD, etc.
- ○ Restaurant gift certificate
- ○ Movie passes
- ○ Other: ....

"If we are going to hold employees accountable for their shortcomings, we have to also hold them accountable for their achievements."

–ADRIAN GOSTICK and **CHESTER ELTON,** *authors*

Don't forget to record this recognition moment in the Employee Log.

ADDITIONAL NOTES

PRESENTATION PREPARATION

Name/Event: ....

Date: ....

Value being recognized: ....

Tell a story using SAIL

✳ Situation *(the problem or opportunity)*:

....

....

....

....

✳ Action *(what was done, in specific terms)*:

....

....

....

....

✳ Impact *(the result of the action)*:

....

....

....

....

✳ Link *(how the action contributed to the company)*:

....

....

....

....

RECOGNITION GIVEN

Recognition ideas:

○ Handwritten thank-you note

○ Company performance recognition award

○ Personalized certificate or plaque

○ Training class or seminar

○ Event ticket (sports or arts)

○ Media: DVD, CD, etc.

○ Restaurant gift certificate

○ Movie passes

○ Other: ....

Don't forget to record this recognition moment in the Employee Log.

ADDITIONAL NOTES

PRESENTATION PREPARATION

Name/Event: ....

Date: ....

Value being recognized: ....

Tell a story using SAIL

  *   Situation *(the problem or opportunity)*:

....

....

....

....

  *   Action *(what was done, in specific terms)*:

....

....

....

....

  *   Impact *(the result of the action)*:

....

....

....

....

  *   Link *(how the action contributed to the company)*:

....

....

....

....

RECOGNITION GIVEN

Recognition ideas:

- ○ Handwritten thank-you note
- ○ Company performance recognition award
- ○ Personalized certificate or plaque
- ○ Training class or seminar

- ○ Event ticket (sports or arts)
- ○ Media: DVD, CD, etc.
- ○ Restaurant gift certificate
- ○ Movie passes
- ○ Other: ....

"People work for the money but go the extra mile for recognition, praise, and rewards."

—STUART LEVINE, *former CEO, Dale Carnegie & Associates*

Don't forget to record this recognition moment in the Employee Log.

ADDITIONAL NOTES

PRESENTATION PREPARATION

Name/Event: ....

Date: ....

Value being recognized: ....

Tell a story using SAIL

✱ Situation *(the problem or opportunity)*:

....

....

....

....

✱ Action *(what was done, in specific terms)*:

....

....

....

....

✱ Impact *(the result of the action)*:

....

....

....

....

✱ Link *(how the action contributed to the company)*:

....

....

....

....

RECOGNITION GIVEN

Recognition ideas:

○ Handwritten thank-you note

○ Company performance
 recognition award

○ Personalized certificate
 or plaque

○ Training class or seminar

○ Event ticket (sports or arts)

○ Media: DVD, CD, etc.

○ Restaurant gift certificate

○ Movie passes

○ Other: ....

Don't forget to record this recognition moment in the Employee Log.

ADDITIONAL NOTES

PRESENTATION PREPARATION

Name/Event: ....

Date: ....

Value being recognized: ....

Tell a story using SAIL

　　✱　Situation *(the problem or opportunity)*:

....

....

....

....

　　✱　Action *(what was done, in specific terms)*:

....

....

....

....

　　✱　Impact *(the result of the action)*:

....

....

....

....

　　✱　Link *(how the action contributed to the company)*:

....

....

....

....

RECOGNITION GIVEN

Recognition ideas:

- Handwritten thank-you note
- Company performance recognition award
- Personalized certificate or plaque
- Training class or seminar

- Event ticket (sports or arts)
- Media: DVD, CD, etc.
- Restaurant gift certificate
- Movie passes
- Other: ....

"When it comes to recognition, one size definitely does *not* fit all. Recognition must be personalized to employee interests, needs, and preferences."

—ADRIAN GOSTICK and CHESTER ELTON, *authors*

Don't forget to record this recognition moment in the Employee Log.

ADDITIONAL NOTES

PRESENTATION PREPARATION

Name/Event: ....

Date: ....

Value being recognized: ....

Tell a story using SAIL

* Situation *(the problem or opportunity)*:

....

....

....

....

* Action *(what was done, in specific terms)*:

....

....

....

....

* Impact *(the result of the action)*:

....

....

....

....

* Link *(how the action contributed to the company)*:

....

....

....

....

RECOGNITION GIVEN

Recognition ideas:

- ○ Handwritten thank-you note
- ○ Company performance recognition award
- ○ Personalized certificate or plaque
- ○ Training class or seminar

- ○ Event ticket (sports or arts)
- ○ Media: DVD, CD, etc.
- ○ Restaurant gift certificate
- ○ Movie passes
- ○ Other: ....

 Don't forget to record this recognition moment in the Employee Log.

ADDITIONAL NOTES

PRESENTATION PREPARATION

Name/Event: ....

Date: ....

Value being recognized: ....

Tell a story using SAIL

    ＊ Situation *(the problem or opportunity)*:

....

....

....

....

    ＊ Action *(what was done, in specific terms)*:

....

....

....

....

    ＊ Impact *(the result of the action)*:

....

....

....

....

    ＊ Link *(how the action contributed to the company)*:

....

....

....

....

RECOGNITION GIVEN

Recognition ideas:

- ○   Handwritten thank-you note
- ○   Company performance recognition award
- ○   Personalized certificate or plaque
- ○   Training class or seminar

- ○   Event ticket (sports or arts)
- ○   Media: DVD, CD, etc.
- ○   Restaurant gift certificate
- ○   Movie passes
- ○   Other: ....

"Giving people a chance to be 'visible' for their work and accomplishments is the smartest thing a manager can do to motivate them."

–BITS AND PIECES, *publication of* The Economic Press

Don't forget to record this recognition moment in the Employee Log.

ADDITIONAL NOTES

PRESENTATION PREPARATION

Name/Event: ....

Date: ....

Value being recognized: ....

Tell a story using SAIL

    ✳ Situation *(the problem or opportunity)*:

....

....

....

....

    ✳ Action *(what was done, in specific terms)*:

....

....

....

....

    ✳ Impact *(the result of the action)*:

....

....

....

....

    ✳ Link *(how the action contributed to the company)*:

....

....

....

....

RECOGNITION GIVEN

Recognition ideas:

○ Handwritten thank-you note

○ Company performance recognition award

○ Personalized certificate or plaque

○ Training class or seminar

○ Event ticket (sports or arts)

○ Media: DVD, CD, etc.

○ Restaurant gift certificate

○ Movie passes

○ Other: ....

Don't forget to record this recognition moment in the Employee Log.

ADDITIONAL NOTES

PRESENTATION PREPARATION

Name/Event: ....

Date: ....

Value being recognized: ....

Tell a story using SAIL

✳ Situation *(the problem or opportunity)*:

....

....

....

....

✳ Action *(what was done, in specific terms)*:

....

....

....

....

✳ Impact *(the result of the action)*:

....

....

....

....

✳ Link *(how the action contributed to the company)*:

....

....

....

....

RECOGNITION GIVEN

Recognition ideas:

- ○ Handwritten thank-you note
- ○ Company performance recognition award
- ○ Personalized certificate or plaque
- ○ Training class or seminar

- ○ Event ticket (sports or arts)
- ○ Media: DVD, CD, etc.
- ○ Restaurant gift certificate
- ○ Movie passes
- ○ Other: ....

> "As a leader, it's important to remember that specific, frequent praise isn't the warm and fuzzy side of life, it's an essential component of leadership."
>
> **–ADRIAN GOSTICK** and **CHESTER ELTON,** *authors*

Don't forget to record this recognition moment in the Employee Log.

ADDITIONAL NOTES

PRESENTATION PREPARATION

Name/Event: ....

Date: ....

Value being recognized: ....

Tell a story using SAIL

✱   Situation *(the problem or opportunity)*:

....

....

....

....

✱   Action *(what was done, in specific terms)*:

....

....

....

....

✱   Impact *(the result of the action)*:

....

....

....

....

✱   Link *(how the action contributed to the company)*:

....

....

....

....

RECOGNITION GIVEN

Recognition ideas:

- Handwritten thank-you note
- Company performance recognition award
- Personalized certificate or plaque
- Training class or seminar

- Event ticket (sports or arts)
- Media: DVD, CD, etc.
- Restaurant gift certificate
- Movie passes
- Other: ....

Don't forget to record this recognition moment in the Employee Log.

ADDITIONAL NOTES

PRESENTATION PREPARATION

Name/Event: ....

Date: ....

Value being recognized: ....

Tell a story using SAIL

* Situation *(the problem or opportunity)*:

....

....

....

....

* Action *(what was done, in specific terms)*:

....

....

....

....

* Impact *(the result of the action)*:

....

....

....

....

* Link *(how the action contributed to the company)*:

....

....

....

....

RECOGNITION GIVEN

Recognition ideas:

- ○ Handwritten thank-you note
- ○ Company performance recognition award
- ○ Personalized certificate or plaque
- ○ Training class or seminar

- ○ Event ticket (sports or arts)
- ○ Media: DVD, CD, etc.
- ○ Restaurant gift certificate
- ○ Movie passes
- ○ Other: ....

"Appreciative words are the most powerful force for good on Earth!"

–GEORGE W. CRANE, *publisher*

Don't forget to record this recognition moment in the Employee Log.

ADDITIONAL NOTES

PRESENTATION PREPARATION

Name/Event: ....

Date: ....

Value being recognized: ....

Tell a story using SAIL

*   Situation *(the problem or opportunity)*:

....

....

....

....

*   Action *(what was done, in specific terms)*:

....

....

....

....

*   Impact *(the result of the action)*:

....

....

....

....

*   Link *(how the action contributed to the company)*:

....

....

....

....

RECOGNITION GIVEN

Recognition ideas:

- ○ Handwritten thank-you note
- ○ Company performance recognition award
- ○ Personalized certificate or plaque
- ○ Training class or seminar

- ○ Event ticket (sports or arts)
- ○ Media: DVD, CD, etc.
- ○ Restaurant gift certificate
- ○ Movie passes
- ○ Other: ....

Don't forget to record this recognition moment in the Employee Log.

PRESENTATION PREPARATION

Name/Event: ....

Date: ....

Value being recognized: ....

Tell a story using SAIL

* Situation *(the problem or opportunity)*:

....

....

....

....

* Action *(what was done, in specific terms)*:

....

....

....

....

* Impact *(the result of the action)*:

....

....

....

....

* Link *(how the action contributed to the company)*:

....

....

....

....

RECOGNITION GIVEN

Recognition ideas:

- Handwritten thank-you note
- Company performance recognition award
- Personalized certificate or plaque
- Training class or seminar

- Event ticket (sports or arts)
- Media: DVD, CD, etc.
- Restaurant gift certificate
- Movie passes
- Other: ....

A survey of more than 33,000 award recipients revealed that the award presentation affects employees' perceptions of not only the award but the entire company.

–O.C. TANNER SURVEY

Don't forget to record this recognition moment in the Employee Log.

ADDITIONAL NOTES

PRESENTATION PREPARATION

Name/Event: ....

Date: ....

Value being recognized: ....

Tell a story using SAIL

✳ Situation *(the problem or opportunity)*:

....

....

....

....

✳ Action *(what was done, in specific terms)*:

....

....

....

....

✳ Impact *(the result of the action)*:

....

....

....

....

✳ Link *(how the action contributed to the company)*:

....

....

....

....

RECOGNITION GIVEN

Recognition ideas:

○ Handwritten thank-you note	○ Event ticket (sports or arts)
○ Company performance recognition award	○ Media: DVD, CD, etc.
	○ Restaurant gift certificate
○ Personalized certificate or plaque	○ Movie passes
○ Training class or seminar	○ Other: ....

 Don't forget to record this recognition moment in the Employee Log.

ADDITIONAL NOTES

PRESENTATION PREPARATION

Name/Event: ....

Date: ....

Value being recognized: ....

Tell a story using SAIL

    *   Situation *(the problem or opportunity)*:

....

....

....

....

    *   Action *(what was done, in specific terms)*:

....

....

....

....

    *   Impact *(the result of the action)*:

....

....

....

....

    *   Link *(how the action contributed to the company)*:

....

....

....

....

RECOGNITION GIVEN

Recognition ideas:

○ Handwritten thank-you note

○ Company performance
recognition award

○ Personalized certificate
or plaque

○ Training class or seminar

○ Event ticket (sports or arts)

○ Media: DVD, CD, etc.

○ Restaurant gift certificate

○ Movie passes

○ Other: ....

"One of the most effective ways to motivate known to man is one of most simple: a compliment."

–ADRIAN GOSTICK and CHESTER ELTON, *authors*

Don't forget to record this recognition moment in the Employee Log.

ADDITIONAL NOTES

PRESENTATION PREPARATION

Name/Event: ....

Date: ....

Value being recognized: ....

Tell a story using SAIL

✱ Situation *(the problem or opportunity)*:

....

....

....

....

✱ Action *(what was done, in specific terms)*:

....

....

....

....

✱ Impact *(the result of the action)*:

....

....

....

....

✱ Link *(how the action contributed to the company)*:

....

....

....

....

RECOGNITION GIVEN

Recognition ideas:

- ○ Handwritten thank-you note
- ○ Company performance recognition award
- ○ Personalized certificate or plaque
- ○ Training class or seminar

- ○ Event ticket (sports or arts)
- ○ Media: DVD, CD, etc.
- ○ Restaurant gift certificate
- ○ Movie passes
- ○ Other:

 Don't forget to record this recognition moment in the Employee Log.

ADDITIONAL NOTES

PRESENTATION PREPARATION

Name/Event: ....

Date: ....

Value being recognized: ....

Tell a story using SAIL

* Situation *(the problem or opportunity)*:

....

....

....

....

* Action *(what was done, in specific terms)*:

....

....

....

....

* Impact *(the result of the action)*:

....

....

....

....

* Link *(how the action contributed to the company)*:

....

....

....

....

RECOGNITION GIVEN

Recognition ideas:

- Handwritten thank-you note
- Company performance recognition award
- Personalized certificate or plaque
- Training class or seminar

- Event ticket (sports or arts)
- Media: DVD, CD, etc.
- Restaurant gift certificate
- Movie passes
- Other: ....

"People don't leave companies, they leave managers."

—GALLUP

Don't forget to record this recognition moment in the Employee Log.

ADDITIONAL NOTES

PRESENTATION PREPARATION

Name/Event: ....

Date: ....

Value being recognized: ....

Tell a story using SAIL

✱ Situation *(the problem or opportunity)*:

....

....

....

....

✱ Action *(what was done, in specific terms)*:

....

....

....

....

✱ Impact *(the result of the action)*:

....

....

....

....

✱ Link *(how the action contributed to the company)*:

....

....

....

....

RECOGNITION GIVEN

Recognition ideas:

- ○ Handwritten thank-you note
- ○ Company performance recognition award
- ○ Personalized certificate or plaque
- ○ Training class or seminar
- ○ Event ticket (sports or arts)
- ○ Media: DVD, CD, etc.
- ○ Restaurant gift certificate
- ○ Movie passes
- ○ Other: ....

Don't forget to record this recognition moment in the Employee Log.

ADDITIONAL NOTES

PRESENTATION PREPARATION

Name/Event:...

Date:...

Value being recognized:...

Tell a story using SAIL

    ✳   Situation *(the problem or opportunity):*

....
....
....
....

    ✳   Action *(what was done, in specific terms):*

....
....
....
....

    ✳   Impact *(the result of the action):*

....
....
....
....

    ✳   Link *(how the action contributed to the company):*

....
....
....
....

RECOGNITION GIVEN

Recognition ideas:

- ○ Handwritten thank-you note
- ○ Company performance recognition award
- ○ Personalized certificate or plaque
- ○ Training class or seminar

- ○ Event ticket (sports or arts)
- ○ Media: DVD, CD, etc.
- ○ Restaurant gift certificate
- ○ Movie passes
- ○ Other: ....

"Outstanding leaders go out of their way to boost the self-esteem of their personnel. If people believe in themselves, it is amazing what they can accomplish."

–SAM WALTON, *founder, Wal-Mart*

Don't forget to record this recognition moment in the Employee Log.

ADDITIONAL NOTES

PRESENTATION PREPARATION

Name/Event: ....

Date: ....

Value being recognized: ....

Tell a story using SAIL

✶ Situation *(the problem or opportunity)*:

....

....

....

....

✶ Action *(what was done, in specific terms)*:

....

....

....

....

✶ Impact *(the result of the action)*:

....

....

....

....

✶ Link *(how the action contributed to the company)*:

....

....

....

....

RECOGNITION GIVEN

Recognition ideas:

- ○ Handwritten thank-you note
- ○ Company performance recognition award
- ○ Personalized certificate or plaque
- ○ Training class or seminar

- ○ Event ticket (sports or arts)
- ○ Media: DVD, CD, etc.
- ○ Restaurant gift certificate
- ○ Movie passes
- ○ Other: ....

Don't forget to record this recognition moment in the Employee Log.

ADDITIONAL NOTES

PRESENTATION PREPARATION

Name/Event: ....

Date: ....

Value being recognized: ....

Tell a story using SAIL

* Situation *(the problem or opportunity)*:

....

....

....

....

* Action *(what was done, in specific terms)*:

....

....

....

....

* Impact *(the result of the action)*:

....

....

....

....

* Link *(how the action contributed to the company)*:

....

....

....

....

RECOGNITION GIVEN

Recognition ideas:

- ○ Handwritten thank-you note
- ○ Company performance recognition award
- ○ Personalized certificate or plaque
- ○ Training class or seminar

- ○ Event ticket (sports or arts)
- ○ Media: DVD, CD, etc.
- ○ Restaurant gift certificate
- ○ Movie passes
- ○ Other: ....

"Gone are the days when people stay because they love their organization. Today, great people stay because they love the people they work for."

−ADRIAN GOSTICK and CHESTER ELTON, *authors*

Don't forget to record this recognition moment in the Employee Log.

ADDITIONAL NOTES

PRESENTATION PREPARATION

Name/Event: ....

Date: ....

Value being recognized: ....

Tell a story using SAIL

* Situation *(the problem or opportunity)*:

....

....

....

....

* Action *(what was done, in specific terms)*:

....

....

....

....

* Impact *(the result of the action)*:

....

....

....

....

* Link *(how the action contributed to the company)*:

....

....

....

....

RECOGNITION GIVEN

Recognition ideas:

○ Handwritten thank-you note

○ Company performance recognition award

○ Personalized certificate or plaque

○ Training class or seminar

○ Event ticket (sports or arts)

○ Media: DVD, CD, etc.

○ Restaurant gift certificate

○ Movie passes

○ Other: ....

Don't forget to record this recognition moment in the Employee Log.

ADDITIONAL NOTES

PRESENTATION PREPARATION

Name/Event: ....

Date: ....

Value being recognized: ....

Tell a story using SAIL

    *   Situation *(the problem or opportunity)*:

....

....

....

....

    *   Action *(what was done, in specific terms)*:

....

....

....

....

    *   Impact *(the result of the action)*:

....

....

....

....

    *   Link *(how the action contributed to the company)*:

....

....

....

....

RECOGNITION GIVEN

Recognition ideas:

- ○ Handwritten thank-you note
- ○ Company performance recognition award
- ○ Personalized certificate or plaque
- ○ Training class or seminar

- ○ Event ticket (sports or arts)
- ○ Media: DVD, CD, etc.
- ○ Restaurant gift certificate
- ○ Movie passes
- ○ Other: ....

"At McDonald's, we believe carrots come in many forms. We believe in treating employees with respect, communicating openly, celebrating successes, and saying 'thanks' for a job well done."

–BILL JOHNSON, *president and CEO, McDonald's Canada*

Don't forget to record this recognition moment in the Employee Log.

ADDITIONAL NOTES

PRESENTATION PREPARATION

Name/Event: ....

Date: ....

Value being recognized: ....

Tell a story using SAIL

* Situation *(the problem or opportunity)*:

....

....

....

....

* Action *(what was done, in specific terms)*:

....

....

....

....

* Impact *(the result of the action)*:

....

....

....

....

* Link *(how the action contributed to the company)*:

....

....

....

....

RECOGNITION GIVEN

Recognition ideas:

- ○ Handwritten thank-you note
- ○ Company performance recognition award
- ○ Personalized certificate or plaque
- ○ Training class or seminar

- ○ Event ticket (sports or arts)
- ○ Media: DVD, CD, etc.
- ○ Restaurant gift certificate
- ○ Movie passes
- ○ Other: ....

Don't forget to record this recognition moment in the Employee Log.

ADDITIONAL NOTES

PRESENTATION PREPARATION

Name/Event: ....

Date: ....

Value being recognized: ....

Tell a story using SAIL

✱ Situation *(the problem or opportunity)*:

....

....

....

....

✱ Action *(what was done, in specific terms)*:

....

....

....

....

✱ Impact *(the result of the action)*:

....

....

....

....

✱ Link *(how the action contributed to the company)*:

....

....

....

....

RECOGNITION GIVEN

Recognition ideas:

- ○ Handwritten thank-you note
- ○ Company performance recognition award
- ○ Personalized certificate or plaque
- ○ Training class or seminar
- ○ Event ticket (sports or arts)
- ○ Media: DVD, CD, etc.
- ○ Restaurant gift certificate
- ○ Movie passes
- ○ Other: ....

"You have to be able to listen well if you are going to motivate the people who work for you."

–LEE IACOCCA, *American industrialist*

Don't forget to record this recognition moment in the Employee Log.

ADDITIONAL NOTES

PRESENTATION PREPARATION

Name/Event: ....

Date: ....

Value being recognized: ....

Tell a story using SAIL

> ✳ Situation *(the problem or opportunity)*:

....

....

....

....

> ✳ Action *(what was done, in specific terms)*:

....

....

....

....

> ✳ Impact *(the result of the action)*:

....

....

....

....

> ✳ Link *(how the action contributed to the company)*:

....

....

....

....

RECOGNITION GIVEN

Recognition ideas:

- ○ Handwritten thank-you note
- ○ Company performance recognition award
- ○ Personalized certificate or plaque
- ○ Training class or seminar

- ○ Event ticket (sports or arts)
- ○ Media: DVD, CD, etc.
- ○ Restaurant gift certificate
- ○ Movie passes
- ○ Other: ....

Don't forget to record this recognition moment in the Employee Log.

PRESENTATION PREPARATION

Name/Event: ....

Date: ....

Value being recognized: ....

Tell a story using SAIL

* Situation *(the problem or opportunity)*:

....

....

....

....

* Action *(what was done, in specific terms)*:

....

....

....

....

* Impact *(the result of the action)*:

....

....

....

....

* Link *(how the action contributed to the company)*:

....

....

....

....

RECOGNITION GIVEN

Recognition ideas:

- ○ Handwritten thank-you note
- ○ Company performance recognition award
- ○ Personalized certificate or plaque
- ○ Training class or seminar

- ○ Event ticket (sports or arts)
- ○ Media: DVD, CD, etc.
- ○ Restaurant gift certificate
- ○ Movie passes
- ○ Other: ....

"Our biggest achievements come while lifting someone else into the spotlight."

–ADRIAN GOSTICK and CHESTER ELTON, *authors*

Don't forget to record this recognition moment in the Employee Log.

ADDITIONAL NOTES

PRESENTATION PREPARATION

Name/Event: ....

Date: ....

Value being recognized: ....

Tell a story using SAIL

✱ Situation *(the problem or opportunity)*:

....

....

....

....

✱ Action *(what was done, in specific terms)*:

....

....

....

....

✱ Impact *(the result of the action)*:

....

....

....

....

✱ Link *(how the action contributed to the company)*:

....

....

....

....

RECOGNITION GIVEN

Recognition ideas:

○ Handwritten thank-you note

○ Company performance
  recognition award

○ Personalized certificate
  or plaque

○ Training class or seminar

○ Event ticket (sports or arts)

○ Media: DVD, CD, etc.

○ Restaurant gift certificate

○ Movie passes

○ Other: ....

Don't forget to record this recognition moment in the Employee Log.

ADDITIONAL NOTES

PRESENTATION PREPARATION

Name/Event: ....

Date: ....

Value being recognized: ....

Tell a story using SAIL

* Situation *(the problem or opportunity)*:

....
....
....
....

* Action *(what was done, in specific terms)*:

....
....
....
....

* Impact *(the result of the action)*:

....
....
....
....

* Link *(how the action contributed to the company)*:

....
....
....
....

RECOGNITION GIVEN

Recognition ideas:

- ○ Handwritten thank-you note
- ○ Company performance recognition award
- ○ Personalized certificate or plaque
- ○ Training class or seminar

- ○ Event ticket (sports or arts)
- ○ Media: DVD, CD, etc.
- ○ Restaurant gift certificate
- ○ Movie passes
- ○ Other: ....

Society for Human Resource Management statistics show that 79 percent of people leave their jobs due to lack of recognition.

Don't forget to record this recognition moment in the Employee Log.

PRESENTATION PREPARATION

Name/Event: ....

Date: ....

Value being recognized: ....

Tell a story using SAIL

    ✳ Situation *(the problem or opportunity)*:

....

....

....

....

    ✳ Action *(what was done, in specific terms)*:

....

....

....

....

    ✳ Impact *(the result of the action)*:

....

....

....

....

    ✳ Link *(how the action contributed to the company)*:

....

....

....

....

RECOGNITION GIVEN

Recognition ideas:

○ Handwritten thank-you note

○ Company performance
recognition award

○ Personalized certificate
or plaque

○ Training class or seminar

○ Event ticket (sports or arts)

○ Media: DVD, CD, etc.

○ Restaurant gift certificate

○ Movie passes

○ Other: ....

Don't forget to record this recognition moment in the Employee Log.

ADDITIONAL NOTES

PRESENTATION PREPARATION

Name/Event: ....

Date: ....

Value being recognized: ....

Tell a story using SAIL

* Situation *(the problem or opportunity)*:

....

....

....

....

* Action *(what was done, in specific terms)*:

....

....

....

....

* Impact *(the result of the action)*:

....

....

....

....

* Link *(how the action contributed to the company)*:

....

....

....

....

RECOGNITION GIVEN

Recognition ideas:

- ○ Handwritten thank-you note
- ○ Company performance recognition award
- ○ Personalized certificate or plaque
- ○ Training class or seminar
- ○ Event ticket (sports or arts)
- ○ Media: DVD, CD, etc.
- ○ Restaurant gift certificate
- ○ Movie passes
- ○ Other: ....

"There are as many ways to recognize people as there are people to recognize. You just have to use your brain to find them. Next time you think you've exhausted the possibilities, THINK AGAIN . . . !"

–ERIC HARVEY, *author,* 180 Ways to Walk the Recognition Talk

Don't forget to record this recognition moment in the Employee Log.

ADDITIONAL NOTES

PRESENTATION PREPARATION

Name/Event: ....

Date: ....

Value being recognized: ....

Tell a story using SAIL

    ✳ Situation *(the problem or opportunity)*:

....

....

....

....

    ✳ Action *(what was done, in specific terms)*:

....

....

....

....

    ✳ Impact *(the result of the action)*:

....

....

....

....

    ✳ Link *(how the action contributed to the company)*:

....

....

....

....

RECOGNITION GIVEN

Recognition ideas:

- Handwritten thank-you note
- Company performance recognition award
- Personalized certificate or plaque
- Training class or seminar

- Event ticket (sports or arts)
- Media: DVD, CD, etc.
- Restaurant gift certificate
- Movie passes
- Other: ....

Don't forget to record this recognition moment in the Employee Log.

PRESENTATION PREPARATION

Name/Event: ....

Date: ....

Value being recognized: ....

Tell a story using SAIL

    ✱ Situation *(the problem or opportunity)*:

....

....

....

....

    ✱ Action *(what was done, in specific terms)*:

....

....

....

....

    ✱ Impact *(the result of the action)*:

....

....

....

....

    ✱ Link *(how the action contributed to the company)*:

....

....

....

....

RECOGNITION GIVEN

Recognition ideas:

- Handwritten thank-you note
- Company performance recognition award
- Personalized certificate or plaque
- Training class or seminar

- Event ticket (sports or arts)
- Media: DVD, CD, etc.
- Restaurant gift certificate
- Movie passes
- Other: ....

"Recognition is a great communicator. . . . By recognizing people, they see the business is doing okay. And best of all, it helps set the standards of what my expectations are."

–JOHN A. BYRNE, *editor in chief,* Fast Company *magazine*

Don't forget to record this recognition moment in the Employee Log.

ADDITIONAL NOTES

PRESENTATION PREPARATION

Name/Event: ....

Date: ....

Value being recognized: ....

Tell a story using SAIL

    ✱   Situation *(the problem or opportunity)*:

....

....

....

....

    ✱   Action *(what was done, in specific terms)*:

....

....

....

....

    ✱   Impact *(the result of the action)*:

....

....

....

....

    ✱   Link *(how the action contributed to the company)*:

....

....

....

....

RECOGNITION GIVEN

Recognition ideas:

○ Handwritten thank-you note

○ Company performance recognition award

○ Personalized certificate or plaque

○ Training class or seminar

○ Event ticket (sports or arts)

○ Media: DVD, CD, etc.

○ Restaurant gift certificate

○ Movie passes

○ Other: ....

 Don't forget to record this recognition moment in the Employee Log.

ADDITIONAL NOTES

PRESENTATION PREPARATION

Name/Event: ....

Date: ....

Value being recognized: ....

Tell a story using SAIL

✱   Situation *(the problem or opportunity)*:

....

....

....

....

✱   Action *(what was done, in specific terms)*:

....

....

....

....

✱   Impact *(the result of the action)*:

....

....

....

....

✱   Link *(how the action contributed to the company)*:

....

....

....

....

RECOGNITION GIVEN

Recognition ideas:

- ○ Handwritten thank-you note
- ○ Company performance recognition award
- ○ Personalized certificate or plaque
- ○ Training class or seminar

- ○ Event ticket (sports or arts)
- ○ Media: DVD, CD, etc.
- ○ Restaurant gift certificate
- ○ Movie passes
- ○ Other:.....................................

"When high-impact performers are asked why they left an organization, many report, 'No one ever asked me to stay!'"

–MARSHALL GOLDSMITH, *founding director, Alliance for Strategic Leadership*

 Don't forget to record this recognition moment in the Employee Log.

ADDITIONAL NOTES

PRESENTATION PREPARATION

Name/Event: ....

Date: ....

Value being recognized: ....

Tell a story using SAIL

*   Situation *(the problem or opportunity):*

....

....

....

....

*   Action *(what was done, in specific terms):*

....

....

....

....

*   Impact *(the result of the action):*

....

....

....

....

*   Link *(how the action contributed to the company):*

....

....

....

....

RECOGNITION GIVEN

Recognition ideas:

- ○ Handwritten thank-you note
- ○ Company performance recognition award
- ○ Personalized certificate or plaque
- ○ Training class or seminar

- ○ Event ticket (sports or arts)
- ○ Media: DVD, CD, etc.
- ○ Restaurant gift certificate
- ○ Movie passes
- ○ Other: ....

 Don't forget to record this recognition moment in the Employee Log.

ADDITIONAL NOTES

PRESENTATION PREPARATION

Name/Event: ....

Date: ....

Value being recognized: ....

Tell a story using SAIL

✱   Situation *(the problem or opportunity)*:

....

....

....

....

✱   Action *(what was done, in specific terms)*:

....

....

....

....

✱   Impact *(the result of the action)*:

....

....

....

....

✱   Link *(how the action contributed to the company)*:

....

....

....

....

RECOGNITION GIVEN

Recognition ideas:

- ○ Handwritten thank-you note
- ○ Company performance recognition award
- ○ Personalized certificate or plaque
- ○ Training class or seminar

- ○ Event ticket (sports or arts)
- ○ Media: DVD, CD, etc.
- ○ Restaurant gift certificate
- ○ Movie passes
- ○ Other: ....

"People are like wells. When they give and give and give their best ideas and get little or nothing in return, they run dry."

–ADRIAN GOSTICK and CHESTER ELTON, *authors*

 Don't forget to record this recognition moment in the Employee Log.

ADDITIONAL NOTES

PRESENTATION PREPARATION

Name/Event: ....

Date: ....

Value being recognized: ....

Tell a story using SAIL

* Situation *(the problem or opportunity)*:

....

....

....

....

* Action *(what was done, in specific terms)*:

....

....

....

....

* Impact *(the result of the action)*:

....

....

....

....

* Link *(how the action contributed to the company)*:

....

....

....

....

RECOGNITION GIVEN

Recognition ideas:

- ○ Handwritten thank-you note
- ○ Company performance recognition award
- ○ Personalized certificate or plaque
- ○ Training class or seminar

- ○ Event ticket (sports or arts)
- ○ Media: DVD, CD, etc.
- ○ Restaurant gift certificate
- ○ Movie passes
- ○ Other: ....

 Don't forget to record this recognition moment in the Employee Log.

PRESENTATION PREPARATION

Name/Event: ....

Date: ....

Value being recognized: ....

Tell a story using SAIL

    ✳ Situation *(the problem or opportunity)*:

....

....

....

....

    ✳ Action *(what was done, in specific terms)*:

....

....

....

....

    ✳ Impact *(the result of the action)*:

....

....

....

....

    ✳ Link *(how the action contributed to the company)*:

....

....

....

....

RECOGNITION GIVEN

Recognition ideas:

- ○ Handwritten thank-you note
- ○ Company performance recognition award
- ○ Personalized certificate or plaque
- ○ Training class or seminar
- ○ Event ticket (sports or arts)
- ○ Media: DVD, CD, etc.
- ○ Restaurant gift certificate
- ○ Movie passes
- ○ Other:...

"Listen with your full attention, look for the good in others, have a sense of humor, and say 'thank you' for a job well done."

–PAUL SMUCKER, *former CEO, The J.M. Smucker Company*

Don't forget to record this recognition moment in the Employee Log.

ADDITIONAL NOTES

PRESENTATION PREPARATION

Name/Event: ....

Date: ....

Value being recognized: ....

Tell a story using SAIL

   ✳ Situation *(the problem or opportunity)*:

....

....

....

....

   ✳ Action *(what was done, in specific terms)*:

....

....

....

....

   ✳ Impact *(the result of the action)*:

....

....

....

....

   ✳ Link *(how the action contributed to the company)*:

....

....

....

....

RECOGNITION GIVEN

Recognition ideas:

- ○ Handwritten thank-you note
- ○ Company performance recognition award
- ○ Personalized certificate or plaque
- ○ Training class or seminar

- ○ Event ticket (sports or arts)
- ○ Media: DVD, CD, etc.
- ○ Restaurant gift certificate
- ○ Movie passes
- ○ Other: ....

Don't forget to record this recognition moment in the Employee Log.

ADDITIONAL NOTES

PRESENTATION PREPARATION

Name/Event: ....

Date: ....

Value being recognized: ....

Tell a story using SAIL

    ✱ Situation *(the problem or opportunity)*:

....

....

....

....

    ✱ Action *(what was done, in specific terms)*:

....

....

....

....

    ✱ Impact *(the result of the action)*:

....

....

....

....

    ✱ Link *(how the action contributed to the company)*:

....

....

....

....

RECOGNITION GIVEN

Recognition ideas:

○ Handwritten thank-you note	○ Event ticket (sports or arts)
○ Company performance recognition award	○ Media: DVD, CD, etc.
	○ Restaurant gift certificate
○ Personalized certificate or plaque	○ Movie passes
○ Training class or seminar	○ Other: ....

"Recognition is America's most underused motivational tool."

–RICHARD KOVACEVICH, *chairman and CEO, Wells Fargo*

 Don't forget to record this recognition moment in the Employee Log.

ADDITIONAL NOTES

PRESENTATION PREPARATION

Name/Event: ....

Date: ....

Value being recognized: ....

Tell a story using SAIL

✳ Situation *(the problem or opportunity)*:

....

....

....

....

✳ Action *(what was done, in specific terms)*:

....

....

....

....

✳ Impact *(the result of the action)*:

....

....

....

....

✳ Link *(how the action contributed to the company)*:

....

....

....

....

RECOGNITION GIVEN

Recognition ideas:

- ○ Handwritten thank-you note
- ○ Company performance recognition award
- ○ Personalized certificate or plaque
- ○ Training class or seminar

- ○ Event ticket (sports or arts)
- ○ Media: DVD, CD, etc.
- ○ Restaurant gift certificate
- ○ Movie passes
- ○ Other: ....

Don't forget to record this recognition moment in the Employee Log.

ADDITIONAL NOTES

PRESENTATION PREPARATION

Name/Event: ....

Date: ....

Value being recognized: ....

Tell a story using SAIL

    ✱   Situation *(the problem or opportunity)*:

....

....

....

....

    ✱   Action *(what was done, in specific terms)*:

....

....

....

....

    ✱   Impact *(the result of the action)*:

....

....

....

....

    ✱   Link *(how the action contributed to the company)*:

....

....

....

....

RECOGNITION GIVEN

Recognition ideas:

- ○ Handwritten thank-you note
- ○ Company performance recognition award
- ○ Personalized certificate or plaque
- ○ Training class or seminar

- ○ Event ticket (sports or arts)
- ○ Media: DVD, CD, etc.
- ○ Restaurant gift certificate
- ○ Movie passes
- ○ Other: ....

When 1,010 people were asked what they did with their last cash bonus, almost 30 percent answered that they paid the bills; 18 percent said they couldn't remember.

–AMERICAN EXPRESS SURVEY

Don't forget to record this recognition moment in the Employee Log.

ADDITIONAL NOTES

PRESENTATION PREPARATION

Name/Event: ....

Date: ....

Value being recognized: ....

Tell a story using SAIL

    ✱ Situation *(the problem or opportunity)*:

....

....

....

....

    ✱ Action *(what was done, in specific terms)*:

....

....

....

....

    ✱ Impact *(the result of the action)*:

....

....

....

....

    ✱ Link *(how the action contributed to the company)*:

....

....

....

....

RECOGNITION GIVEN

Recognition ideas:

- Handwritten thank-you note
- Company performance recognition award
- Personalized certificate or plaque
- Training class or seminar

- Event ticket (sports or arts)
- Media: DVD, CD, etc.
- Restaurant gift certificate
- Movie passes
- Other: ....

 Don't forget to record this recognition moment in the Employee Log.

ADDITIONAL NOTES

PRESENTATION PREPARATION

Name/Event: ....

Date: ....

Value being recognized: ....

Tell a story using SAIL

* Situation *(the problem or opportunity)*:

....

....

....

....

* Action *(what was done, in specific terms)*:

....

....

....

....

* Impact *(the result of the action)*:

....

....

....

....

* Link *(how the action contributed to the company)*:

....

....

....

....

RECOGNITION GIVEN

Recognition ideas:

- ○ Handwritten thank-you note
- ○ Company performance recognition award
- ○ Personalized certificate or plaque
- ○ Training class or seminar

- ○ Event ticket (sports or arts)
- ○ Media: DVD, CD, etc.
- ○ Restaurant gift certificate
- ○ Movie passes
- ○ Other:...

"Reward what you want repeated."

–ADRIAN GOSTICK and **CHESTER ELTON,** *authors*

Don't forget to record this recognition moment in the Employee Log.

ADDITIONAL NOTES

PRESENTATION PREPARATION

Name/Event: ....

Date: ....

Value being recognized: ....

Tell a story using SAIL

 ✱ Situation *(the problem or opportunity)*:

....

....

....

....

 ✱ Action *(what was done, in specific terms)*:

....

....

....

....

 ✱ Impact *(the result of the action)*:

....

....

....

....

 ✱ Link *(how the action contributed to the company)*:

....

....

....

....

RECOGNITION GIVEN

Recognition ideas:

- ○ Handwritten thank-you note
- ○ Company performance recognition award
- ○ Personalized certificate or plaque
- ○ Training class or seminar

- ○ Event ticket (sports or arts)
- ○ Media: DVD, CD, etc.
- ○ Restaurant gift certificate
- ○ Movie passes
- ○ Other: ....

Don't forget to record this recognition moment in the Employee Log.

ADDITIONAL NOTES

PRESENTATION PREPARATION

Name/Event: ....

Date: ....

Value being recognized: ....

Tell a story using SAIL

    ✳   Situation *(the problem or opportunity)*:

....

....

....

....

    ✳   Action *(what was done, in specific terms)*:

....

....

....

....

    ✳   Impact *(the result of the action)*:

....

....

....

....

    ✳   Link *(how the action contributed to the company)*:

....

....

....

....

RECOGNITION GIVEN

Recognition ideas:

- ○ Handwritten thank-you note
- ○ Company performance recognition award
- ○ Personalized certificate or plaque
- ○ Training class or seminar

- ○ Event ticket (sports or arts)
- ○ Media: DVD, CD, etc.
- ○ Restaurant gift certificate
- ○ Movie passes
- ○ Other: ....

"The worst mistake a boss can make is not to say 'well done.'"

–JOHN ASHCROFT, *British industrialist*

Don't forget to record this recognition moment in the Employee Log.

ADDITIONAL NOTES

PRESENTATION PREPARATION

Name/Event: ....

Date: ....

Value being recognized: ....

Tell a story using SAIL

* Situation *(the problem or opportunity)*:

....
....
....
....

* Action *(what was done, in specific terms)*:

....
....
....
....

* Impact *(the result of the action)*:

....
....
....
....

* Link *(how the action contributed to the company)*:

....
....
....
....

RECOGNITION GIVEN

Recognition ideas:

- ○ Handwritten thank-you note
- ○ Company performance recognition award
- ○ Personalized certificate or plaque
- ○ Training class or seminar

- ○ Event ticket (sports or arts)
- ○ Media: DVD, CD, etc.
- ○ Restaurant gift certificate
- ○ Movie passes
- ○ Other: ....

Don't forget to record this recognition moment in the Employee Log.

ADDITIONAL NOTES

PRESENTATION PREPARATION

Name/Event: ....

Date: ....

Value being recognized: ....

Tell a story using SAIL

* Situation *(the problem or opportunity)*:

....

....

....

....

* Action *(what was done, in specific terms)*:

....

....

....

....

* Impact *(the result of the action)*:

....

....

....

....

* Link *(how the action contributed to the company)*:

....

....

....

....

RECOGNITION GIVEN

Recognition ideas:

- ○ Handwritten thank-you note
- ○ Company performance recognition award
- ○ Personalized certificate or plaque
- ○ Training class or seminar

- ○ Event ticket (sports or arts)
- ○ Media: DVD, CD, etc.
- ○ Restaurant gift certificate
- ○ Movie passes
- ○ Other: ....

"A sincere thank-you doesn't come from a well-written script but from a sincere heart. Don't worry that the words aren't elegant; just make sure the feeling is right."

–ADRIAN GOSTICK and CHESTER ELTON, *authors*

Don't forget to record this recognition moment in the Employee Log.

ADDITIONAL NOTES

PRESENTATION PREPARATION

Name/Event: ....

Date: ....

Value being recognized: ....

Tell a story using SAIL

* Situation *(the problem or opportunity)*:

....

....

....

....

* Action *(what was done, in specific terms)*:

....

....

....

....

* Impact *(the result of the action)*:

....

....

....

....

* Link *(how the action contributed to the company)*:

....

....

....

....

RECOGNITION GIVEN

Recognition ideas:

- ○ Handwritten thank-you note
- ○ Company performance recognition award
- ○ Personalized certificate or plaque
- ○ Training class or seminar

- ○ Event ticket (sports or arts)
- ○ Media: DVD, CD, etc.
- ○ Restaurant gift certificate
- ○ Movie passes
- ○ Other: ....

Don't forget to record this recognition moment in the Employee Log.

ADDITIONAL NOTES

PRESENTATION PREPARATION

Name/Event: ....

Date: ....

Value being recognized: ....

Tell a story using SAIL

*   Situation *(the problem or opportunity)*:

....

....

....

....

*   Action *(what was done, in specific terms)*:

....

....

....

....

*   Impact *(the result of the action)*:

....

....

....

....

*   Link *(how the action contributed to the company)*:

....

....

....

....

RECOGNITION GIVEN

Recognition ideas:

- ○ Handwritten thank-you note
- ○ Company performance recognition award
- ○ Personalized certificate or plaque
- ○ Training class or seminar

- ○ Event ticket (sports or arts)
- ○ Media: DVD, CD, etc.
- ○ Restaurant gift certificate
- ○ Movie passes
- ○ Other: ....

"Attention employers: Make sure your employees feel valued. Otherwise, they could bolt for other jobs as soon as the economy starts to improve."

–JANE KIM, Wall Street Journal

 Don't forget to record this recognition moment in the Employee Log.

ADDITIONAL NOTES

PRESENTATION PREPARATION

Name/Event: ....

Date: ....

Value being recognized: ....

Tell a story using SAIL

* Situation *(the problem or opportunity)*:

....

....

....

....

* Action *(what was done, in specific terms)*:

....

....

....

....

* Impact *(the result of the action)*:

....

....

....

....

* Link *(how the action contributed to the company)*:

....

....

....

....

RECOGNITION GIVEN

Recognition ideas:

- ○ Handwritten thank-you note
- ○ Company performance recognition award
- ○ Personalized certificate or plaque
- ○ Training class or seminar

- ○ Event ticket (sports or arts)
- ○ Media: DVD, CD, etc.
- ○ Restaurant gift certificate
- ○ Movie passes
- ○ Other:..

 Don't forget to record this recognition moment in the Employee Log.

ADDITIONAL NOTES

PRESENTATION PREPARATION

Name/Event: ....

Date: ....

Value being recognized: ....

Tell a story using SAIL

✳ Situation *(the problem or opportunity)*:

....

....

....

....

✳ Action *(what was done, in specific terms)*:

....

....

....

....

✳ Impact *(the result of the action)*:

....

....

....

....

✳ Link *(how the action contributed to the company)*:

....

....

....

....

RECOGNITION GIVEN

Recognition ideas:

- ○ Handwritten thank-you note
- ○ Company performance recognition award
- ○ Personalized certificate or plaque
- ○ Training class or seminar
- ○ Event ticket (sports or arts)
- ○ Media: DVD, CD, etc.
- ○ Restaurant gift certificate
- ○ Movie passes
- ○ Other: ....

"**Great management is born when recognition is added to the core characteristics of leadership: goal setting, communication, trust, and accountability.**"

–**ADRIAN GOSTICK** and **CHESTER ELTON,** *authors*

Don't forget to record this recognition moment in the Employee Log.

ADDITIONAL NOTES

PRESENTATION PREPARATION

Name/Event: ....

Date: ....

Value being recognized: ....

Tell a story using SAIL

✱   Situation *(the problem or opportunity)*:

....

....

....

....

✱   Action *(what was done, in specific terms)*:

....

....

....

....

✱   Impact *(the result of the action)*:

....

....

....

....

✱   Link *(how the action contributed to the company)*:

....

....

....

....

RECOGNITION GIVEN

Recognition ideas:

- Handwritten thank-you note
- Company performance recognition award
- Personalized certificate or plaque
- Training class or seminar

- Event ticket (sports or arts)
- Media: DVD, CD, etc.
- Restaurant gift certificate
- Movie passes
- Other:..

 Don't forget to record this recognition moment in the Employee Log.

ADDITIONAL NOTES

EMPLOYEE LOG

Fill out these questionnaires by interviewing each employee to best recognize his or her above-and-beyond performances. Ask each person how he or she wants to be recognized. Each individual prefers to be recognized in different ways (i.e. some prefer to be recognized in a public celebration; others prefer quiet, personal recognition; etc.).

Employee Name: _____

What type of celebration does this person prefer? *(Check all that apply.)*

○ Quiet   ○ Formal

○ Party   ○ Other: ....

....

What formal recognition would he/she like? *(Check all that apply.)*

○ Company performance   ○ Something with the
   recognition award   company logo

○ Framed certificate of   ○ Other: ....
   achievement   ....

○ Engraved plaque or other   ....
   memento

If this person had a free day, have him/her describe what he/she would do
and where he/she would go: ....

....

....

....

....

....

Would he/she want the accomplishment publicized?

○ Yes   ○ No

What type of day-to-day recognition would he/she appreciate?
(Check all that apply.)

○ Handwritten thank-you note   ○ Concert ticket

○ Typed letter for personnel file   ○ Movie pass

○ Training class or seminar   ○ Restaurant gift certificate

○ CD or DVD   ○ Shopping gift card

○ Ticket to a sporting event   ○ Other: ....

Who would he/she prefer to present an award?

○ Person who nominated him/   ○ Senior management
her for the award

Employee-specific list:

	DATE	RECOGNITION
1		
2		
3		
4		
5		
6		
7		
8		
9		
10		

Employee Name: _____

What type of celebration does this person prefer? *(Check all that apply.)*

○ Quiet

○ Party

○ Formal

○ Other: ....

What formal recognition would he/she like? *(Check all that apply.)*

○ Company performance recognition award

○ Framed certificate of achievement

○ Engraved plaque or other memento

○ Something with the company logo

○ Other: ....
....
....

If this person had a free day, have him/her describe what he/she would do and where he/she would go: ....
....
....
....
....
....

Would he/she want the accomplishment publicized?

○ Yes

○ No

What type of day-to-day recognition would he/she appreciate?
(Check all that apply.)

- ○ Handwritten thank-you note
- ○ Typed letter for personnel file
- ○ Training class or seminar
- ○ CD or DVD
- ○ Ticket to a sporting event

- ○ Concert ticket
- ○ Movie pass
- ○ Restaurant gift certificate
- ○ Shopping gift card
- ○ Other: ....

Who would he/she prefer to present an award?

- ○ Person who nominated him/ her for the award
- ○ Senior management

Employee-specific list:

	DATE	RECOGNITION
1		
2		
3		
4		
5		
6		
7		
8		
9		
10		

Employee Name: _____

What type of celebration does this person prefer? *(Check all that apply.)*

○ Quiet

○ Party

○ Formal

○ Other: ....

What formal recognition would he/she like? *(Check all that apply.)*

○ Company performance recognition award

○ Framed certificate of achievement

○ Engraved plaque or other memento

○ Something with the company logo

○ Other: ....

....

....

If this person had a free day, have him/her describe what he/she would do and where he/she would go: ....

....

....

....

....

....

Would he/she want the accomplishment publicized?

○ Yes

○ No

What type of day-to-day recognition would he/she appreciate?
(Check all that apply.)

- ○ Handwritten thank-you note
- ○ Typed letter for personnel file
- ○ Training class or seminar
- ○ CD or DVD
- ○ Ticket to a sporting event

- ○ Concert ticket
- ○ Movie pass
- ○ Restaurant gift certificate
- ○ Shopping gift card
- ○ Other: ....

Who would he/she prefer to present an award?

- ○ Person who nominated him/ her for the award
- ○ Senior management

Employee-specific list:

	DATE	RECOGNITION
1		
2		
3		
4		
5		
6		
7		
8		
9		
10		

Employee Name: _____

What type of celebration does this person prefer? *(Check all that apply.)*

○ Quiet ○ Formal

○ Party ○ Other: ....

What formal recognition would he/she like? *(Check all that apply.)*

○ Company performance recognition award

○ Something with the company logo

○ Framed certificate of achievement

○ Other: ....

○ Engraved plaque or other memento

If this person had a free day, have him/her describe what he/she would do and where he/she would go: ....

....

....

....

....

....

Would he/she want the accomplishment publicized?

○ Yes ○ No

What type of day-to-day recognition would he/she appreciate?
(Check all that apply.)

○ Handwritten thank-you note   ○ Concert ticket

○ Typed letter for personnel file   ○ Movie pass

○ Training class or seminar   ○ Restaurant gift certificate

○ CD or DVD   ○ Shopping gift card

○ Ticket to a sporting event   ○ Other: ....

Who would he/she prefer to present an award?

○ Person who nominated him/   ○ Senior management
  her for the award

Employee-specific list:

	DATE	RECOGNITION
1		
2		
3		
4		
5		
6		
7		
8		
9		
10		

Employee Name: _____

What type of celebration does this person prefer? *(Check all that apply.)*

○ Quiet

○ Party

○ Formal

○ Other: _____

....

What formal recognition would he/she like? *(Check all that apply.)*

○ Company performance recognition award

○ Framed certificate of achievement

○ Engraved plaque or other memento

○ Something with the company logo

○ Other: _____
_____

_____

If this person had a free day, have him/her describe what he/she would do and where he/she would go: _____

....

....

....

....

....

Would he/she want the accomplishment publicized?

○ Yes

○ No

What type of day-to-day recognition would he/she appreciate?
(Check all that apply.)

- ○ Handwritten thank-you note
- ○ Typed letter for personnel file
- ○ Training class or seminar
- ○ CD or DVD
- ○ Ticket to a sporting event

- ○ Concert ticket
- ○ Movie pass
- ○ Restaurant gift certificate
- ○ Shopping gift card
- ○ Other: ....

Who would he/she prefer to present an award?

- ○ Person who nominated him/ her for the award
- ○ Senior management

Employee-specific list:

	DATE	RECOGNITION
1		
2		
3		
4		
5		
6		
7		
8		
9		
10		

Employee Name: _____

What type of celebration does this person prefer? *(Check all that apply.)*

○ Quiet   ○ Formal

○ Party   ○ Other:_____

....

What formal recognition would he/she like? *(Check all that apply.)*

○ Company performance   ○ Something with the
  recognition award   company logo

○ Framed certificate of   ○ Other:_____
  achievement
                             ....

○ Engraved plaque or other
  memento   ....

If this person had a free day, have him/her describe what he/she would do
and where he/she would go: ....

....

....

....

....

....

Would he/she want the accomplishment publicized?

○ Yes   ○ No

What type of day-to-day recognition would he/she appreciate?
(Check all that apply.)

- ○ Handwritten thank-you note
- ○ Typed letter for personnel file
- ○ Training class or seminar
- ○ CD or DVD
- ○ Ticket to a sporting event

- ○ Concert ticket
- ○ Movie pass
- ○ Restaurant gift certificate
- ○ Shopping gift card
- ○ Other:...

Who would he/she prefer to present an award?

- ○ Person who nominated him/ her for the award
- ○ Senior management

Employee-specific list:

	DATE	RECOGNITION
1		
2		
3		
4		
5		
6		
7		
8		
9		
10		

Employee Name: _____

What type of celebration does this person prefer? *(Check all that apply.)*

○ Quiet   ○ Formal

○ Party   ○ Other: ....

What formal recognition would he/she like? *(Check all that apply.)*

○ Company performance recognition award   ○ Something with the company logo

○ Framed certificate of achievement   ○ Other: ....

○ Engraved plaque or other memento

If this person had a free day, have him/her describe what he/she would do and where he/she would go: ....

....

....

....

....

....

Would he/she want the accomplishment publicized?

○ Yes   ○ No

What type of day-to-day recognition would he/she appreciate?
(Check all that apply.)

○ Handwritten thank-you note   ○ Concert ticket

○ Typed letter for personnel file   ○ Movie pass

○ Training class or seminar   ○ Restaurant gift certificate

○ CD or DVD   ○ Shopping gift card

○ Ticket to a sporting event   ○ Other: ....

Who would he/she prefer to present an award?

○ Person who nominated him/   ○ Senior management
    her for the award

Employee-specific list:

	DATE	RECOGNITION
1		
2		
3		
4		
5		
6		
7		
8		
9		
10		

Employee Name: _____

What type of celebration does this person prefer? *(Check all that apply.)*

○ Quiet

○ Party

○ Formal

○ Other: ....

....

What formal recognition would he/she like? *(Check all that apply.)*

○ Company performance recognition award

○ Framed certificate of achievement

○ Engraved plaque or other memento

○ Something with the company logo

○ Other: ....

....

....

If this person had a free day, have him/her describe what he/she would do and where he/she would go: ....

....

....

....

....

....

Would he/she want the accomplishment publicized?

○ Yes

○ No

What type of day-to-day recognition would he/she appreciate?
(Check all that apply.)

○ Handwritten thank-you note   ○ Concert ticket

○ Typed letter for personnel file   ○ Movie pass

○ Training class or seminar   ○ Restaurant gift certificate

○ CD or DVD   ○ Shopping gift card

○ Ticket to a sporting event   ○ Other:..

Who would he/she prefer to present an award?

○ Person who nominated him/   ○ Senior management
her for the award

Employee-specific list:

	DATE	RECOGNITION
1		
2		
3		
4		
5		
6		
7		
8		
9		
10		

Employee Name: _____

What type of celebration does this person prefer? *(Check all that apply.)*

○ Quiet

○ Party

○ Formal

○ Other: _____

What formal recognition would he/she like? *(Check all that apply.)*

○ Company performance recognition award

○ Framed certificate of achievement

○ Engraved plaque or other memento

○ Something with the company logo

○ Other: _____

_____

_____

If this person had a free day, have him/her describe what he/she would do and where he/she would go: ....

....

....

....

....

....

Would he/she want the accomplishment publicized?

○ Yes

○ No

What type of day-to-day recognition would he/she appreciate?
(Check all that apply.)

- ○ Handwritten thank-you note
- ○ Typed letter for personnel file
- ○ Training class or seminar
- ○ CD or DVD
- ○ Ticket to a sporting event

- ○ Concert ticket
- ○ Movie pass
- ○ Restaurant gift certificate
- ○ Shopping gift card
- ○ Other: ....

Who would he/she prefer to present an award?

- ○ Person who nominated him/ her for the award
- ○ Senior management

Employee-specific list:

	DATE	RECOGNITION
1		
2		
3		
4		
5		
6		
7		
8		
9		
10		

Employee Name: _____

What type of celebration does this person prefer? *(Check all that apply.)*

- ○ Quiet
- ○ Party

- ○ Formal
- ○ Other: ....

What formal recognition would he/she like? *(Check all that apply.)*

- ○ Company performance recognition award
- ○ Framed certificate of achievement
- ○ Engraved plaque or other memento

- ○ Something with the company logo
- ○ Other: ....
  ....
  ....

If this person had a free day, have him/her describe what he/she would do and where he/she would go: ....

....

....

....

....

....

Would he/she want the accomplishment publicized?

- ○ Yes
- ○ No

What type of day-to-day recognition would he/she appreciate?
(Check all that apply.)

○ Handwritten thank-you note   ○ Concert ticket

○ Typed letter for personnel file   ○ Movie pass

○ Training class or seminar   ○ Restaurant gift certificate

○ CD or DVD   ○ Shopping gift card

○ Ticket to a sporting event   ○ Other: ....

Who would he/she prefer to present an award?

○ Person who nominated him/   ○ Senior management
    her for the award

Employee-specific list:

	DATE	RECOGNITION
1		
2		
3		
4		
5		
6		
7		
8		
9		
10